CHILDHOOD

An Anthology of Verse and Prose

CHILDHOOD

An Anthology of Verse and Prose

LORENZ BOOKS

LONDON • NEW YORK • SYDNEY • BATH

First published in 1996 by Lorenz Books

Lorenz Books is an imprint of
Anness Publishing Limited
1 Boundary Row
London SE1 8HP

Distributed in Canada by Raincoast Books Distribution Limited

ISBN 1 85967 291 4

A CIP catalogue record is available from the British Library

Publisher: Joanna Lorenz
Consultant Editor: Rosie Hankin
Managing Editor: Helen Sudell
Designer: Bet Ayer

Printed in Singapore by Star Standard Industries Pte. Ltd.

Contents

Babes and Sucklings

Here we have a baby. It is composed
of a bald head and a pair of lungs.

EUGENE FIELD (1850-95)
from *The Tribune Primer*

Child of My love, "Lean Hard,"
And let Me feel the pressure of thy care.
I know thy burden, child; I shaped it,
Poised it in Mine own hand, made no proportion
Of its weight to thine unaided strength;
For even as I laid it on I said -
I shall be near, and while she leans on Me,
This burden shall be Mine, not hers;
So shall I keep My child within the circling arms
Of Mine own love. Here lay it down, nor fear
To impose it on a shoulder which upholds
The government of worlds. Yet closer come,
Thou art not near enough; I would embrace thy care,
So I might feel My child reposing on My breast.
Thou lovest Me? I know it. Doubt not then,
But, loving Me, lean hard.

CHARLOTTE BICKERSTETH WARD (1860-1922)
Lean Hard

Her, by her smile, how soon the stranger knows;
How soon by his the glad discovery shows,
As to her lips she lifts the lovely boy,
What answering looks of sympathy and joy!
He walks, he speaks. In many a broken word,
His wants, his wishes, and his griefs are heard.
And ever, ever to her lap he flies,
When rosy sleep comes on with sweet surprise.
Locked in her arms, his arms across her flung
(That name most dear for ever on his tongue),
As with soft accents round her neck he clings,
And, cheek to cheek, her lulling song she sings:
How blest to feel the beatings of his heart,
Breathe his sweet breath, and bliss for bliss impart:
Watch o'er his slumbers like the brooding dove,
And, if she can, exhaust a mother's love.

SAMUEL ROGERS (1773-1855)
A Mother's Love

Come, my little one, with me!
There are wondrous sights to see
As the evening shadows fall;
In your pretty cap and gown,
Don't detain -
The Shut-Eye train -
"Ting-a-ling!" the bell it goeth,
"Toot-toot!" the whistle bloweth,
And we hear the warning call:
"All aboard for Shut-Eye Town!"

Over hill and over plain
Soon will speed the Shut-Eye train!
Through the blue where bloom the stars
And the Mother Moon looks down
We'll away
To land of Fay -
Oh, the sights that we shall see there!
Come, my little one, with me there -
'Tis a goodly train of cars -
All aboard for Shut-Eye Town!

Shut-Eye Town is passing fair -
Golden dreams await us there;
We shall dream those dreams, my dear
Till the mother Moon goes down -
See unfold
Delights untold!
And in those mysterious places
We shall see beloved faces
And beloved voices hear
In the grace of Shut-Eye Town.

Heavy are your eyes, my sweet,
Weary are your little feet -
Nestle closer up to me
In your pretty cap and gown;
Don't detain
The Shut-Eye train!
"Ting-a-ling!" the bell it goeth,
"Toot-toot!" the whistle bloweth,
Oh, the sights that we shall see!
All aboard for Shut-Eye Town!

EUGENE FIELD (1850-95)
The Shut-Eye Train

12

There was a time when I was very small
When my whole frame was but an ell in height;
Sweetly, as I recall it, tears do fall,
And therefore I recall it with delight.

I sported in my tender mother's arms,
And rode a-horseback on best father's knee;
Alike were sorrows, passions and alarms,
And gold, and Greek, and love, unknown to me.

JENS IMMANUEL BAGGESEN (1764-1826)
Childhood

14

I was a little stranger, which, at my entrance into the world, was saluted and surrounded with innumerable joys. My knowledge was divine ... My very ignorance was advantageous. I seemed as one brought into the Estate of Innocence. All things were spotless and pure and glorious: yea, and infinitely mine, and joyful and precious. I knew not that there were any sins, or complaints or laws. I dreamed not of poverties, contentions or vices. All tears and quarrels were hidden from mine eyes. Everything was at rest, free and immortal. I knew nothing of sickness or death or rents or exaction, either for tribute or bread. In the absence of these I was entertained like an angel with the works of God in their splendour and glory, I saw all in the peace of Eden; heaven and earth did sing my Creator's praises, and could not make more melody to Adam than to me. All time was eternity, and a perpetual Sabbath. Is it not strange that an infant should be heir of the whole world, and see those mysteries which the books of the learned never unfold?

THOMAS TRAHERNE (1637-74)
Estate of Innocence from "Centuries of Meditations" published 1908 (written c. 1670)

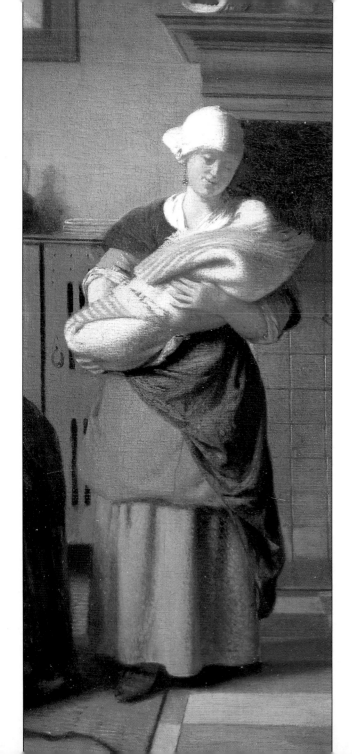

Sweet babe! true portrait of thy father's face,
  Sleep on the bosom that thy lips have pressed!
Sleep, little one; and closely, gently place
  Thy drowsy eyelid on thy mother's breast.

Upon that tender eye, my little friend,
  Soft sleep shall come, that cometh not to me!
I watch to see thee, nourish thee, defend;
  'Tis sweet to watch for thee, alone for thee!

His arms fall down; sleep sits upon his brow;
  His eye is closed; he sleeps, nor dreams of harm.
Wore not his cheek the apple's ruddy glow,
  Would you not say he slept on Death's cold arm?

Awake, my boy! I tremble with affright!
  Awake, and chase this fatal thought! Unclose
Thine eye but for one moment on the light!
  Even at the price of thine, give me repose!

Sweet error! he but slept, I breathe again;
  Come, gentle dreams, the hour of sleep beguile!
O, when shall he, for whom I sigh in vain,
  Beside me watch to see thy waking smile?

HENRY WADSWORTH LONGFELLOW (1807-82)
The Child Asleep

To Be A Child

The childhood shows the man
As morning shows the day.

JOHN MILTON (1608-74)

Know you what it is to be a child? It is to be something very different from the man of to-day. It is to have a spirit yet streaming from the waters of baptism; it is to believe in love, to believe in loveliness, to believe in belief; it is to be so little that the elves can reach to whisper in your ear; it is to turn pumpkins into coaches, and mice into horses, lowness into loftiness, and nothing into everything, for each child has its fairy godmother in its soul.

FRANCIS THOMPSON (1859-1907)

Monday's child is fair of face,
Tuesday's child is full of grace,
Wednesday's child is full of woe,
Thursday's child has far to go,
Friday's child is loving and giving,
Saturday's child works hard for his living,
But a child that is born on the Sabbath day
Is fair and wise and good and gay.

ANON

I remember, I remember
  The house where I was born,
The little window where the sun
  Came peeping in at morn;
He never came a wink too soon
  Nor brought too long a day;
But now, I often wish the night
  Had borne my breath away.

I remember, I remember
  The roses, red and white,
The violets, and the lily-cups –
  Those flowers made of light!
The lilacs where the robin built,
  And where my brother set
The laburnum on his birthday –
  The tree is living yet!

I remember, I remember
  Where I once used to swing,
And thought the air must rush as fresh
  To swallows on the wing;
My spirit flew in feathers then,
  That is so heavy now,
And summer pools could hardly cool
  The fever on my brow.

I remember, I remember
  The fir trees dark and high;
I used to think their slender tops
  Were close against the sky;
It was a childish ignorance,
  But now 'tis little joy
To know I'm farther off from Heav'n
  Than when I was a boy.

THOMAS HOOD (1835-74)
I remember, I remember

Airy, fairy Lilian,
  Flitting, fairy Lilian,
When I ask her if she love me,
Claps her tiny hands above me,
  Laughing all she can;
She'll not tell me if she love me,
  Cruel little Lilian.

ALFRED, LORD TENNYSON (1809-92)
from *Lilian*

Blessings on thee, little man,
Barefoot boy, with cheek of tan!
With thy turned-up pantaloons,
And thy merry whistled tunes;
With thy red lip, redder still
Kissed by strawberries on the hill;
With the sunshine on thy face,
Through thy torn brim's jaunty grace;
From my heart I give thee joy, –

I was once a barefoot boy!
Prince thou art, – the grown-up man
Only is republican.
Let the million-dollared ride!
Barefoot, trudging at his side,
Thou hast more than he can buy
In the reach of ear and eye, –
Outward sunshine, inward joy:
Blessings on thee, barefoot boy!

JOHN GREENLEAF WHITTIER (1807-92)
The Barefoot Boy

If mother knew the way I felt –
 And I'm sure a mother should –
She wouldn't make it quite so hard
 For a person to be good!

I want to do the things she says;
 I try to all day long;
And then she just skips all the right,
 And pounces on the wrong!

A dozen times I do a thing,
 And one time I forget;
And then she looks at me and asks
 If I can't remember yet?

She'll tell me to do something,
 And I'll really start to go;
But she'll keep right on telling it
 As if I didn't know,

Till it seems as if I couldn't –
 It makes me kind of wild;
And then she says she never saw
 Such a disobliging child.

I go to bed all sorry,
 And say my prayers, and cry,
And mean next day to be so good
 I just can't wait to try.

And I get up next morning,
 And mean to do just right;
But mother's sure to scold me
 About something before night.

I wonder if she really thinks
 A child could go so far,
As to be perfect all the time
 As the grown-up people are!

If she only knew I tried to –
 And I'm sure a mother should –
She wouldn't make it quite so hard
 For a person to be good!

ANON

29

By day you cannot see the sky
For it is up so very high.
You look and look, but it's so blue
That you can never see right through.

But when night comes it is quite plain,
And all the stars are there again.
They seem just like old friends to me,
I've known them all my life you see.

There is the dipper first, and there
Is Cassiopeia in her chair,
Orion's belt, the Milky Way,
and lots I know but cannot say.

One group looks like a swarm of bees,
Papa says they're the Pleiades;
But I think they must be the toy
Of some nice little angel boy.

Perhaps his jackstones which to-day
He has forgot to put away.
And left them lying on the sky
Where he will find them bye and bye.

I wish he'd come and play with me.
We'd have such fun, for it would be
A most unusual thing for boys
To feel that they had stars for toys!

AMY LOWELL (1874-1925)
The Pleiades

A Widening World

W hen I was a child, I understood as a child,
I thought as a child: but when I became a man,
I put away childish things.

I Corinthians 13, 11

I lie on my back, looking up at the sky
And watch all the different clouds go by,
And wherever they wander, they seem to grow
Like the towns and the country down below.

One is a church with a steeple tall,
And one is a castle, with ruined wall,
One is a mountain, and one a tree –
Or that is the way they look to me.

And there, where a bit of the sky shows through,
Is a valley, that holds a lake of blue;
And that tiniest cloud, that goes so fast
Is a wee little boat, a-sailing past.

I could lie on my back in the grass all day,
And watch while the clouds fly by in play –
I wonder if children I cannot see
Lie up in the clouds and look down at me?

MARY FANNY YOUNGS
Cloud Castles

But soon inured to alphabetic toils,
Alert I met the dame with jocund smiles;
First at the form, my task for ever true,
A little favourite rapidly I grew:

And oft she stroked my head with fond delight,
Held me a pattern to the dunce's sight;
And as she gave my diligence its praise,
Talked of the honours of my future days.

HENRY KIRKE WHITE (1785-1806)
from *The Dame School*

36

" ... I say, Arthur, what a brick your mother is to make us so cosy. But look here, now, you must answer straight up when the fellows speak to you, and don't be afraid. If you're afraid, you'll get bullied. And don't say you can sing; and don't you ever talk about home, or your mother and sisters."

THOMAS HUGHES (1822-96)
from *Tom Brown's School Days*, 1857

She would spend the day prowling round the garden, eating, watching, laughing, picking at the grapes on the vines like a thrush, secretly plucking a peach from the trellis, climbing a plum-tree, or giving it a little surreptitious shake as she passed to bring down a rain of the golden mirabelles which melt in the mouth like scented honey. Or she would pick the flowers, although that was forbidden: quickly she would pluck a rose that she had been coveting all day, and run away with it to the arbour at the end of the garden. Then she would bury her little nose in the delicious-scented flower, and kiss it, and bite it, and suck it: and then she would conceal her booty, and hide it in her bosom between her little breasts, at the wonder of whose coming she would gaze in eager fondness.

ROMAIN ROLLAND (1866-1944)
from *Jean Christophe*, 1904
(translated by Gilbert Cannan)

Tommy Bangs was the scapegrace of the school, and the most trying little scapegrace that ever lived. As full of mischief as a monkey, yet so good-hearted that one could not help forgiving his tricks; so scatter-brained that words went by him like the wind, yet so penitent for every misdeed, that it was impossible to keep sober when he vowed tremendous vows of reformation, or proposed all sorts of queer punishments to be inflicted upon himself. Mr and Mrs Bhaer lived in a state of preparation for any mishap, from the breaking of Tommy's own neck, to the blowing up of the entire family with gunpowder; and Nursey had a particular drawer in which she kept bandages, plasters, and salves for his especial use, for Tommy was always being brought in half-dead; but nothing ever killed him, and he rose from every downfall with redoubled vigour.

The first day he came, he chopped the top off one finger in the hay-cutter, and during the week, fell from the shed roof, was chased by an angry hen who tried to pick his eyes out because he examined her chickens, got run away with, and had his ears boxed violently by Asia, who caught him luxuriously skimming a pan of cream with half a stolen pie. Undaunted, however, by any failures or rebuffs, this indomitable youth went on amusing himself with all sorts of tricks till no one felt safe. If he did not know his lessons, he always had some droll excuse to offer, and as he was usually clever at his books, and as bright as a button in composing answers when he did not know them, he got on pretty well at school. But out of school – Ye gods and little fishes! how Tommy did carouse!

LOUISA M ALCOTT (1832-88)
from *Little Men*, 1871

...If ever I tasted a disembodied transport on earth, it was in those friendships which I entertained at school, before I dreamt of any maturer feeling ... I loved my friend for his gentleness, his candour, his truth, his good repute, his freedom from my own livelier manner, his calm and reasonable kindness. It was not any particular talent that attracted me to him, or anything striking whatsoever. I should say, in one word, it was his goodness. I doubt whether he ever had a conception of a tithe of the regard and respect I entertained for him; and I smile to think of the perplexity (though he never showed it) which he probably felt sometimes at my enthusiastic expressions; for I thought him a kind of angel ... With the other boys I played antics, and rioted in fantastic jests; but in his society, or whenever I thought of him, I fell into a kind of Sabbath state of bliss; and I am sure I could of died for him.

I experienced this delightful affection towards three successive schoolfellows ...

JAMES LEIGH HUNT (1784-1859)
from *Autobiography*, 1850

A Guiding Hand

The best way to make children good
is to make them happy.

OSCAR WILDE (1854-1900)

And a woman who held a babe against her bosom said,

Speak to us of Children.

And he said:

Your children are not your children.

They are the sons and daughters of Life's longing for itself.

They come through you but not from you.

And though they are with you yet they belong not to you.

You may give them your love but not your thoughts.

For they have their own thoughts.

You may house their bodies but not their souls.

For their souls dwell in the house of tomorrow, which you cannot visit, not even in your dreams.

You may strive to be like them, but seek not to make them like you.

For life goes not backward nor tarries with yesterday.

You are the bows from which your children as living arrows are sent forth.

The Archer sees the mark upon the path of the infinite, and He bends you with His might that
    His arrows may go swift and far.

Let your bending in the Archer's hand be for gladness;

For even as He loves the arrow that flies, so He loves also the bow that is stable.

KAHLIL GIBRAN (1883-1931)
Children from 'The Prophet'

And they brought young children to him, that he should touch them: and his disciples rebuked those that brought them.

But when Jesus saw it, he was much displeased, and said unto them, Suffer the little children to come unto me, and forbid them not: for of such is the kingdom of God.

Verily I say unto you, Whosoever shall not receive the kingdom of God as a little child, he shall not enter therein.

And he took them up in his arms, put his hands upon them, and blessed them.

St Mark 10, 13-16

Through the night thy Angels kept
Watch beside me while I slept;
Now the dark has passed away,
Thank thee, Lord, for this new day.

Give me food that I may live;
Every naughtiness forgive;
Keep all evil things away
From thy little child this day.

W CANTON (1845-1926)

One of the greatest benefites that God ever gave me, is, that he sent me so sharpe and severe Parentes ... For when I am in presence of father or mother, whether I speke, kepe silence, sit, stand, or go, eate, drinke, be merie or sad, be sawying, plaiying, dauncing, or doing anie thing els, I must do it, as it were, in soch weight, mesure and number, even so perfitelie as God made the world, else I am so sharpelie taunted, so cruellie threatened, yea presentlie some tymes with pinches, nippes and bobbes, and other waies which I will not name for the honor I beare them ... that I think myself in hell.

LADY JANE GREY (1537-54)

D ance there upon the shore;
What need have you to care
For wind or water's roar?
And tumble out your hair
That the salt drops have wet;
Being young you have not known
The fool's triumph, nor yet
Love lost as soon as won,
Nor the best labourer dead
And all the sheaves to bind.
What need have you to dread
The monstrous crying wind?

W B YEATS (1865-1939)
To a Child Dancing in the Wind

Dear Mamma, if you just could be
   A tiny little girl like me,
And I your mamma, you would see
   How nice I'd be to you.
I'd always let you have your way;
I'd never frown at you and say,
   "You are behaving ill today,
   Such conduct will not do."

I'd always give you jelly cake
For breakfast, and I'd never shake
My head, and say, "You must not take
   So very large a slice."
I'd never say, "My dear, I trust
You will not make me say you must
Eat up your oatmeal": or "The crust
   You'll find, is very nice."

I'd never say, "Well, just a few!"
I'd let you stop your lessons too;
I'd say, "They are too hard for you,
   Poor child, to understand."
I'd put the books and slates away;
You shouldn't do a thing but play,
And have a party every day,
   Ah-h-h! wouldn't that be grand!

SYDNEY DAYRE, MRS COCHRAN, C. 1881
A Lesson for Mamma

Pranks and Plays

Birds in their little nests agree;
And 'tis a shameful sight,
When children of one family
Fall out, and chide, and fight.

ISAAC WATTS (1674-1748)
from *Divine Songs for Children*

And when the sunshine grew strong and lasting, so that the buttercups were thick in the meadows, Silas might be seen in the sunny mid-day, or in the late afternoon when the shadows were lengthening under the hedgerows, strolling out with uncovered head to carry Eppie beyond the Stone-pits to where the flowers grew, till they reached some favourite bank where he could sit down, while Eppie toddled to pluck the flowers, and make remarks to the winged things that murmered happily above the bright petals, calling "Dad-Dad's" attention continually by bringing him flowers. Then she would turn her ear to some sudden bird-note, and Silas learned to please her by making signs of hushed stillness, that they might listen for the note to come again: so that when it came, she set up her small back and laughed with gurgling triumph. Sitting on the banks in this way, Silas began to look for the once familiar herbs again; and as the leaves, with their unchanged outline and markings, lay on his palm, there was a sense of crowding remembrances from which he turned away timidly, taking refuge in Eppie's little world, that lay lightly on his enfeebled spirit.

GEORGE ELIOT (1819-80)
from *Silas Marner*, 1861

Come to me, O ye children!
For I hear you at your play,
And the questions that perplexed me
Have vanished quite away.

In your hearts are the birds and the sunshine,
In your thoughts the brooklet's flow,
But in mine is the wind of Autumn
And the first fall of the snow.

For what are all our contrivings,
And the wisdom of our books,
When compared with your caresses,
And the gladness of your looks?

Ye are better than all the ballads
That ever were sung or said;
For ye are living poems,
And all the rest are dead.

HENRY WADSWORTH LONGFELLOW (1807-82)
Children

I'm a beautiful red, red drum,
And I train with the soldier boys;
As up the street we come,
Wonderful is our noise!
There's Tom, and Jim, and Phil,
And Dick, and Nat, and Fred,
While Widow Cutier's Bill
And I march on ahead,
With a r-r-rat-tat-tat
And a tum-titty-um-tum-tum-
Oh, there's bushels of fun in that
For boys with a little red drum!

EUGENE FIELD (1850-95)
The Drum

How dear to this heart are the scenes of my
    childhood,
When fond recollection presents them to view!
The orchard, the meadow, the deep-tangled wildwood,
And every loved spot which my infancy knew!
The wide-spreading pond, and the mill that stood by it,
The bridge and the rock where the cataract fell,
The cot of my father, the dairy house nigh it,
And e'en the rude bucket that hung in the well –
The old oaken bucket, the iron-bound bucket,
The moss-covered bucket which hung in the well.

That moss-covered vessel I hailed as a treasure,
For often at noon, when returned from the field,
I found it the source of an exquisite pleasure,
The purest and sweetest that nature can yield.
How ardent I seized it, with hands that were glowing,
And quick to the white-pebbled bottom it fell;
Then soon, with the emblem of truth overflowing,
And dripping with coolness, it rose from the well –
The old oaken bucket, the iron-bound bucket,
The moss-covered bucket, arose from the well.

How sweet from the green mossy brim to receive it,
As poised on the curb it inclined to my lips!
Not a full blushing goblet could tempt me to leave it,
The brightest that beauty or revelry sips.
And now, far removed from the loved habitation,
The tear of regret will intrusively swell,
As fancy reverts to my father's plantation,
And sighs for the bucket that hangs in the well —
The old oaken bucket, the iron-bound bucket,
The moss-covered bucket that hangs in the well.

Samuel Woodworth
The Bucket

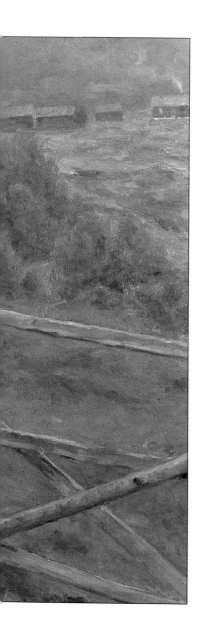

I found an old box hid away in a room,
And, lifting the lid open wide,
I found a little girl's pinafores hid,
And worn-out shoes tucked under the lid,
And tattered old toys inside.

Childhood's dreams all hidden away,
Bits from the "backwoods" lane,
Headless dolls, and a ragged old coat,
And a chokey feeling came into my throat;
I wanted my pinnies again.

I found an old box all hidden away,
Oh, but those were the happiest days!
Pinnies all tattered and hair
    ribbons old,
But somehow I wonder if Heaven
    will hold
The key to my childhood's ways?

ANON
The Old Box

ACKNOWLEDGEMENTS

The Publishers are grateful to the following picture agencies for pictures published in this book.

Bridgeman Art Library, London

Front jacket: *Bathing her Dolls* by Gustav Igler, Josef Mensing Gallery, Hamm-Rhynern. Back jacket: *The Children of Sir Vivian Hussey at the Seaside* by George Elgar Hicks, Roy Miles Gallery, London. p1 *The Lesson* by James Cole, Christopher Wood Gallery, London. p2 *An Impromptu Ball* by Eva Roos, Christie's London. p6 *Motherhood* by Louis Adan, Waterhouse and Dodd, London. p12 *Sleep* by Robert Gemmell Hutchison, City of Edinburgh Museums and Art Galleries. p14 *The First Leap* by Sir Edwin Landseer, Guildhall Art Gallery, Corporation of London. p15 *The Three Sisters* by Johan George Meyer von Bremen, Josef Mensing Gallery, Hamm-Rhynern. p16 *The Christening* by Francis Wheatley, York City Art Gallery. p18 *Nursemaid with baby in an interior and a young girl preparing the cradle* by Pieter de Hooch, Johnny Van Haeften Gallery, London. p20 *Playing Outside the School Room* by Jacob Spoel, Waterhouse and Dodd, London. p21 *Sympathy* by Briton Riviere, Royal Holloway and Bedford New College, Surrey. p23 *A Basket of Flowers* by Jan Brueghel the Elder, Sotheby's, London. p27 *Snap the Whip* by Winslow, Butler Institute of American Art. p28 *Strange Faces* by Frederick Walker, The Fine Art Society, London. p29 *Fillette à l'orange* by Marie Louise Breslau, Victoria & Albert Museum, London. p30 *The Route to School* by Emile Claus, Private Collection. p31 *A Boy Fishing* by Samuel Palmer, Agnew & Sons, London. p32 *Flying the Kite* by Joseph Kirkpatrick, Haworth Art Gallery, Accrington. p33 *Looking at The Dream* by Paul-Emmanuel Legrand, Musee des Beaux-Arts, Nantes/Giraudon. p34 *Spring, 1864* by William McTaggart, National Gallery of Scotland. p36 *The School Room* by Alfred Rankley, Christopher Wood Gallery, London. p37 *Lending a Bite* by William Mulready, Private Collection. p38 *Little Timidity* by Frederick Samuel Beaumont, The Maas Gallery, London. p39 *Early Sorrow* by Louis Lejeune, Royal Holloway & Bedford New College, Surrey. p42 *Lost and Found* by William MacDuff, Christopher Wood Gallery, London. p44 *Scrambling for Cherries* by John Morgan, Atkinson Art Gallery, Southport. p45 *As the twig is bent so is the tree inclined* by James Hayllar, Christopher Wood Gallery, London. *Bathing her Dolls* by Gustav Igler, Josef Mensing

Gallery, Hamm-Rhynem. p48 *Children Playing* by August Malstrom, Nationalmuseum, Stockholm. p52 *Bob Apple* by Frederick Morgan, Rafael Valls Gallery, London. p55 *Playtime* by William Jabez Muckley, Albion Fine Art, London. p56 *Pontus* by Carl Larsson, Nationalmuseum, Stockholm. p57 *Family Worship* from the Pears Annual by Joseph Clark, A & F Pears, Ltd., London. p58 *Happy as the Days are Long* by Frederick Morgan, John Noott Galleries, Broadway. p59 *The Volunteers* by Frederick Daniel Hardy, York City Art Gallery, London. p60 *Feeding the Rabbits* by Charles Edward Wilson, Phillips, The International Fine Art Auctioneers, London. p62 *On the Plain* by Karl Frerick Nordstrom, Goteborgs Konstmuseum, Sweden.

Visual Arts Library, London

Jacket flap: *Bathtime* by Honor Appleton, Chris Beetles Gallery, London. p3 *Sur la Chaise Haute* by Frederick George Cotman. p7 *Sleepy Baby* by Mary Cassat, Dallas Museum of Art. p8 *The Toilet of the Sleepy Child* by Mary Cassat, Los Angeles County Museum. p9 *The Bath* by Mary Cassat, Chicago Art Institute. p10 *Tenement Mother and Children* by Marie Page, Springfield Museum of Art. p11 *Helen Fourment and her Children* by Peter Paul Rubens, Louvre, Paris. p11 *Mrs Vigee le Brun and her daughter* by Vigee le Brun, Louvre, Paris. p13 *Mother and Child* by Mary Cassat, Chicago Art Institute. p22 *Conte de fee* by Tom Browne, Leicester Galleries, London. p24 *Pepito Costa y Bonells* by Fransisco de Goya, New York Metropolitan Museum. p25 *Houshold Task* by Etienne Aubrey, Springfield Museum. p26 *Girl on a Rocking Horse* by Henrietta May Ada Ward, Leicester Galleries, London. p40 *The Great Adventure* by William Henry Hunt, Chris Beetles Gallery, London. p41 *Adam's Ale* by William Henry Hunt, Chris Beetles Gallery, London. p43 *Happy Childhood* by W Homer, Phoenix Art Museum. p46 *Family Group* by Lotto, London National Gallery. p49 *Family Prayer* by P. Fendl, Albertina Gallery, Vienna. p50 *The Family of Jan Bruegel the Elder* by Peter Paul Rubens, Courtauld Gallery, London,. p51 *Miss Murray* by T. Lawrence, Kenwood House, London. p53 *In the Garden* by Morisot, Toledo Museum of Art. p54 *The Seesaw* by Fransisco de Goya, Philadelphia Museum of Art. p61 *Feeding Ducks* by David Woodlock, Chris Beetles Gallery, London. p63 *Young Country Woman Seated with a Stick* by Pissarro, Musee d'Orsay, Paris.